A Halfway House

NEIL POWELL, born in London in 1948, was educated at ... School and the University of Warwick; he has taught English, owned a bookshop and, since 1990, been a full-time author and editor. His books include five previous collections of poetry – *At the Edge* (1977), *A Season of Calm Weather* (1982), *True Colours* (1990), *The Stones on Thorpeness Beach* (1994) and *Selected Poems* (1998) – as well as *Carpenters of Light* (1979), *Roy Fuller: Writer and Society* (1995), *The Language of Jazz* (1997) and *George Crabbe: An English Life* (2004). He lives in Suffolk.

NEIL POWELL

A Halfway House

CARCANET

First published in 2004 by
Carcanet Press Limited
Alliance House
Cross Street
Manchester M2 7AQ

A CIP catalogue record for this book
is available from the British Library

ISBN 1 85754 659 8

The publisher acknowledges financial assistance
from Arts Council England

Set in Monotype Garamond by XL Publishing Services, Tiverton
Printed and bound in England by SRP Ltd, Exeter

For Nick Ash

Contents

1

2

3

4

Acknowledgements

Some of these poems have previously appeared in *The Guardian, The London Magazine, PN Review* and *The Times Literary Supplement*. I originally included 'A Halfway House' as the epilogue to my *Selected Poems* (1998) before realising that it should be the title-poem of a separate book. Three poems in the sequence of epigrams 'The Nature of Things' have had previous lives: 'Books' was in *True Colours* (1991), 'Carcanet' in *A Commonplace Book: Carcanet 1970–2000* (2000) and 'Wheels' was a Mandeville Dragoncard, subsequently broadcast in *Something Understood* (BBC Radio 4). 'The Picture of the Mind' was originally written for an anthology of poems presented to Peter Scupham on his seventieth birthday. Parts of 'The Garden at Clears' and 'Dusk in the Surrey Hills' were written at the Mount Pleasant Writers' Retreat, Coppice Lane, Reigate.

1

My Chelsea

My grandmother lived in a first-floor flat in Chelsea:
10 Limerston Street, a staid unfashionable bit.
She would not have thought of herself as exotic.

But I did, marvelling at her innocent grandeur,
Knowing that she would always be right,
As resonant and inclusive as her radiogram,

Despite odd finds among the ballet highlights:
Black-and-gold Crosbys or magenta Comos
Or, irresistible, Rose Murphy's 'Busy Line'.

Perhaps those were Aunty Cora's, whose name surely
Was that thing for getting middles out of apples
('Where's the Cora?' grumbled mother, rummaging).

But I digress as, inevitably, one does.
My Chelsea was a place at the end of journeys,
Green Southern to Victoria, then the 'inner' Circle –

I'd wonder what had happened to the outer one –
Which sometimes led to Ralph Lee's dental basement
With its buzzing, juddering insect-like black drill:

My mother's childhood dentist and then mine.
How could I guess that in my middle age
He'd gain, at 92, an MBE

For 'services to caravanning'? And sometimes
The journey led instead to Yeoman's Row,
To Freddie's, where my grandmother kept house,

Though what that meant I wasn't sure: only
Not to touch or explore, in spite of which
I'd tinkle on his sweet upright piano,

Until stilled by a gentle voice behind me.
'One day, my boy, you'll make a fine musician.'
I turned to find the choreographer

Smiling shyly. We never met again.
Our lives might intersect – in London, Suffolk –
Yet *in absentia*, the way they do,

Or don't. Perhaps my Chelsea was a place
In which a self might live another life,
The one in which the city didn't sour

Or country snare. We'd walk from Gloucester Road,
South Ken, Sloane Square, or take the 11 bus,
Arriving at a strange, familiar door,

In a street that led to nowhere. 'What's down there?'
I wondered once. 'World's End,' my mother said.
World's *end*? My world had only just begun.

Route 424

We'd catch the 424 from Reigate Station –
Peter, Nigel and I – as if we owned the bus:
First on, grabbing the long back seat upstairs.

We'd made our way through privet-hedged suburbia –
All yappy dogs and frosted-glass front-doors
And signs that said *No Hawkers, No Circulars* –

Across a shrub-mazed roundabout and under
The railway bridge adorned with bad attempts
At genital representation and with comments

Unflattering to our despised headmaster,
Then loitered at the shop in Holmesdale Road
Where, like a mad chemist, white-aproned Mr Dodd

Made brightly coloured test-tube-shaped iced lollies,
Entirely flavourless, but costing a mere penny.
Thus strangely fortified, we'd think ourselves ready

To catch the 424 from Reigate Station,
Rattling down to the Red Cross, High Street, Bell Street
(Where sundry lesser mortals climbed aboard)

Before heaving over Cockshot Hill to Woodhatch:
Nigel lived there, beyond a service road,
In the kind of house you'd only build from Bako –

Thirties, bay-windowed, with a mirror-twin
In an interminable parade of pairs of twins.
I pitied him but, even then, kept quiet about it.

Peter, by contrast, lived at Sidlow Bridge
And by magic could command the bus to stop
Outside his house. He was a sly child

With a mouth like a letterbox, scheming eyes,
And I admired him hugely; what's more, his house
Stood on its own, with outbuildings and grounds.

I fancied myself as an apprentice crim,
Certain that if there was no good to be up to,
Peter would know of it, take me along with him –

Though if he did I have, of course, forgotten.
More likely those were thoughts that lingered in
The darkening upper deck once he'd got off:

As he crossed the road, walked up the drive, I'd look
Over my shoulder – the first friend I'd met
Who seemed to me worth watching out of sight.

And then I'd be alone, dim egg-cupped bulbs
In the curved cream ceiling holding off the dusk,
As lights came on in dolls' house living-rooms,

Where boys like me took off their coats and caps
Or flung down satchels, ravenous for tea.
Now houses gave way to open fields and copses

Until we reached my stop at Irons Bottom;
I'd fetch my bike from Freddy Laker's yard
And ride, down Deanoak Lane, the last mile home.

Results

Saturday teatime: football results slide by,
Unheeded, on the announcer's Brylcreemed voice.

A lightship is moored close to the radio:
Its sails are twin clear bulbs in pallid shades.

Nil's neutral; three or four prompt mild surprise.
Teams fall like skittles: 'League Division Two ...'

My father wants to know 'how Fulham got on';
I'm waiting for *Return to the Lost Planet*.

Meanwhile I'll scan the KB's magic names,
Ranged in pennants on its glowing wavebands:

Green, amber, red, three slim inverted signals.
I light on Allouis, Kalundbourg, Motala:

Are they cities, with castles, dukes and princes,
Or lost tall masts out there in the humming dusk?

The Garden at Clears

'It is closing time in the gardens of the West.'

Cyril Connolly

1

A shingled single track; a broken gate,
Unhinged and folded back against the hedge;
A late spring day in 1958 …
Time hovers like a syrphid at the edge

Of some gigantic leaf: slow minutes pass
As gravel shifts and settles in the lane.
A spider weaves its way among the grass.
The sun is veiled by clouds and clears again.

At length two boys on bicycles arrive
(One is my friend John, the other's me),
Who shade their eyes and squint along the drive:
Two children seeing what there is to see.

But what is there to see? A gate, a track,
Between two grassy fields, a flowering cherry
Disconsolate in blossom's aftershock,
Its fallen petals scattered like confetti;

A wonky board, 'For Sale'. The agent's name
Is 'Powell & Partner': 'Well, that's us,' I say,
And what, a thought ago, had been a game
Acquires the shaping hint of destiny.

The rutted track becomes a path between
Two sloping lawns, untended and unmown;
A landscaped garden shading into green,
Its rockeries and parterres overgrown;

A neat white building locked into the hill.
No one at home: there hasn't been for years.
The house waits in its leafy beauty-sleep
For somebody to reinhabit Clears.

This isn't us, not quite. But John has found
One unlatched window where the upper floor
Comes up against the steeply rising ground,
An open invitation to explore:

And so, my friend and I, we amble through
Rooms where the dusty light of afternoon
Glows on the present's ghostly residue,
Glints at the future. I shall live here soon.

One warm August day, we picnicked in the big back shed
Among the random objects that had yet to find their homes
In still unfurnished rooms.
What had they taken on, what in the world had possessed them,
My parents, to buy this weird house wedged into a hillside
With its untameable acres of landscaped wilderness?
(Later they'd say their ten-year-old son had persuaded them.)
Eating our sandwiches among mangles and mowers,
We felt like the Borrowers:
A giant cotton-reel for a table wouldn't have seemed out of place.

That was the best year, '58–'59,
When I biked to St Mary's, came home for lunch,
A time when lessons were vexatious interruptions
To my life of cycling, roaming the Surrey hills
Or exploring the garden at Clears.
I'd commandeered that big back shed and filled it
With a wind-up gramophone, an ancient typewriter,
And junk purloined from old George Wickens' yard
In Nutley Lane (the Borrowers again).
One day I'd turn up with a box of rare 78s,
The next with a brown rabbit in my saddlebag.

The garden shook off its green surprise and flourished,
Prodigious with bulbs in spring – a drift of snowdrops
Cushioning the dell – and with autumn fruits.
Up a ladder, surrounded by a crowd of feasting wasps,
I picked Tsar plums (there were enough to go round),
Or learned to grasp Blenheims from the highest branches
With a long-handled apple-picker.
The fig trees flapped their elephantine leaves
In fruitless gestures;
Rhubarb stretched out its raw enormous limbs;
Rampant asparagus spread like a dithery, feather-headed weed;
The cute bamboo had grown to an impenetrable copse,
Watched over by a stately copper beech
While, ranged at the end of the lower terraced lawn,
Our landmark team of eleven Lombardy poplars
Stood to ragged attention – with one stump for referee.

How could this ever end? But I went away to school,
Became a boy with a divided soul.

On Boxing Day in '62 it snowed;
It snowed all through the cold new year to Easter.
We put chains on the Wolseley to get along the track
To Colley Lane; the bicycle was useless.
I trekked up to the hills in my huge boots,
Snowballing the friskily silly dog,
The cat in obstinate pursuit, paw-prints chin-deep,
The Shetland ponies more stumpy-legged than ever,
Creamy-brown sheep lined up on the white horizon.
At school, the playing-fields and park were lost in drifts –
We ran on silent, frozen roads –
But when the holidays arrived it was still there, the garden,
Pallid after its long cold storage.

It was the year I discovered West Coast jazz, Stravinsky;
Read Thom Gunn, Iris Murdoch; began to write …
One evening I cycled to the Odeon in Redhill
To see *The Servant*: I was fifteen,
Hungry for experience and bad company,
Gratefully accosted by a man twice my age.
When I got home, my mother, anxious on the landing,
Was waiting up for me: had I enjoyed the film?
Perhaps I'd better not discuss it with my father
Who 'wouldn't really like that sort of thing'.
So many doors closed with the bedroom door;
Then I lay awake, listening to trains in the valley,
A nearby owl and the great immeasurable dark –
Alienated, empowered, and free.
The garden at Clears was growing away from me.

All's fallen into autumn, all's at rest:
The burdened apple-tree, the tangled vine.
It is closing time in the gardens of the West.

Leaves settle slowly into mulch, compressed
As trodden grapes to concentrated wine:
All's fallen into autumn, all's at rest.

We drank the noble vintages, the best;
Now others trickle out their slow decline:
It is closing time in the gardens of the West.

The bird returns to its abandoned nest,
These tattered remnants of a grand design:
All's fallen into autumn, all's at rest,

And dark horizons prove the stormiest.
Thus Connolly in 1949:
'It is closing time in the gardens of the West.'

The written page reverts to palimpsest;
The ink runs white; the letters disentwine.
All's fallen into autumn, all's at rest,
It is closing time in the gardens of the West.

Dusk in the Surrey Hills

Such sly transitions, where lane shades into track,
and track into path, are things that I should know:
like a trick of the light, or a change of key,
or a shift from iambic to syllabic.

And I do know them: here the path limps uphill,
past a dense hedge, a dim mysterious lodge,
and a low field in which a dog stands howling,
while another looks dispassionately on;

two tails wag, and they resume their devotions,
confirming my grateful insignificance;
a rabbit pops up to peer at me, and three
hurrying muntjacs crash past without a glance.

There is pungency in the old rot of yews,
of a past well stewed: its aromatic fug
jostles teasingly with lighter, sharper beech:
a single sniff tells me this is Colley Hill.

Suddenly I'm lost: lostness swoops down like night,
and I realise that what I have mislaid
is not so much the path as the sure instinct
which once would have got me home. Another dog,

this time made of brownish carpet, scuttles by,
taking a dog-sized short-cut no good to me;
and yet, at the next step, my feet find their way,
report back via some forgotten sensory

circuit that these log-faced muddy steps will lead
round a beech-choked crater, and then down again,
where a kind of rustic timbered balustrade
should prevent even the confused from falling.

Strange how panic subsides to knowledge; stranger,
coming from yew-shadow to the last of light
on the path between the fields above The Clears,
to see carpet-dog and owner further on,

in confident possession of their landscape,
striding downhill, where ghostly Shetland ponies
nuzzle the barbed-wire fence, expecting windfalls
from the garden opposite, which once was home.

2

Covehithe

In my dream they said: 'You must go to Covehithe.'
I crossed over the causeway between two blue lakes
And I found myself on a long forest path
With a few wooden shacks and a glimpse of the sea.
I thought after all it was a place that might suit me.
But they said: 'You must learn from your mistakes.'

So, I have come to Covehithe. Low winter sun
Scans fields of pigs, dead skeletal trees,
Collapsing cliffs. There are ships on the horizon.
The great church, wrecked by Civil War, not storm,
Now shields a smaller church from further harm.
And they were wrong: I like it as it is.

Waveney

for Robert Wells

1. Ditchingham Dam

It takes days after rain for the water to rise:
False calm, a fatal illness in remission,
Comforts the sunlit fields. The river sulks;
Then, grumbling, slowly starts to rouse itself;
Barges about, flings upstream vegetation
On tangled banks; and fills to teacup-brim,
Tea-coloured, stirred. Its weather is historic.

And now the meadows soak and bloat like sponges,
Their surface stippled with the tips of grass:
Cattle crowd strange islands; ducks and swans
Find new amazing lakes; across the fields,
The bypass has become a distant shore.
Along the dam, life puts up barricades,
Safe beyond each shut and sandbagged door.

2. The Metfield Imp

He is a tutivillus or a titivil:
His task, to gather up into his sack
Mistakes and mangled words, which he conveys
And scatters on his travels underground.
Thus, if the road to Hell (as Johnson said)
Is paved with good intentions, then this imp
Supplies the paving-slabs: might that explain
His lolling tongue and wide salacious grin?

Perhaps: though if we guessed our errors' value,
Translated into paths for fallen souls,
Would not such faults be easier to assuage?
The imp looks unconvinced: he's heard it all.
Meanwhile, beneath the tower the Metfield Clock,
A broken heart, ticks gravely in its cage.

3. *The Minster*

The past gets lost: we search, research for it
In secret places. Here, at the hidden heart
Of a sacred country, may be where to start,

Or where to end. Still almost out of reach,
Still glossy-guidebook-proof and tourist-free,
Hawthorn and oak and freshly-planted beech

Surround a shadowed clearing and these stones –
A little church for Bishop Herbert, really –
Now bedded down in nettles, celandines.

Thatched, round-ended, with a tall square tower
Is how the artist sees it, yet the Minster
Was disused by the fourteenth century: its power

Lies in that vanishing, that ever-growing
Vacancy. Our knowledge is unknowing.

4. Jane's Island

It reconfigures childhood myths: not Circe,
But *Swallows and Amazons*, *The Wind in the Willows*:
Across a wobbly bridge, this private island
Is where bulbs prosper and ducklings are saved
From becoming carp's breakfasts. A legislature
Unknown to the quotidian world obtains here:
Benign despotism of conservationist, gardener,
Reminds us that 'privilege' means 'private law'.

And a river island seems right for a novelist,
Whose universe is almost like our own,
Though more portably confined. No such luck
For the unterritorial poet; he, ugliest duckling,
Must be tipped off the bank to fend for himself,
Downstream to the staithe and the critical carp.

5. *Across the Bridge*

I once knew a man who was so Suffolk he
Couldn't abide this view across the Waveney:
The sight of Norfolk more than he could stand.
He'd not have been amused to learn I found
In him a match for Joseph Calloway:
That character in Greene's *Across the Bridge*,
Another fraught observer at the edge,
Marooned in Mexico, watching the USA.

Up a lazy river, though not quite the kind
Hoagy Carmichael must have had in mind.
All's lazy here: all residues drift down
This winding street from a sour, shabby town,
Clog at the bridge. Yes, I once knew and know
A man who can't abide this. Time to go.

Reading Proust on Aldeburgh Beach

How near to us they are, these distant children
Whose voices scatter shingle, glance off walls,
Returning. 'You can come in ours, if you like,'
One shouts, pointing at a boat which is not his.

And how such games of vacant possession
Will linger to haunt their deals and their dreams,
In the grey blur of morning, or the fertile dark,
Or the patchwork shadows of late afternoon.

The past, it seems, is not a foreign country,
Nor even down the road in the next town:
It is here and now, at the edge of England,
In children's voices and the arc of a gleam,

Where sunlight and sealight join in the dance
Of images we choose to call remembrance.

A Halfway House

Etched into dusk, it shows we're almost there:
Those lidded windows, biscuit-stucco walls
Between the water-meadows and the sea
Signal exact abandonment. Years drift:
Spring tides engulf it, lapping at the sills;
Gulls claim an apex among missing slates,
Shout their possession from the staring rafters;
Awash all winter, yet on summer nights
The beach will grow through shingle into sand
And turn this place inland.
                        A halfway life
May teach regard for this enduring ruin,
Weathered defender of uncertain ground,
And milestone marking that consoling point
Of nearing home, or starting out again.

1 August 2000

The purple buddleia has outreached itself;
Distended tendrils clog the narrow garden;
Drab blackbirds feed their damp prodigious young;
A wood pigeon calls the cows in after rain.

A quarter century! Its shrubs and birds
Growing, declining in the season's dance,
As I find, baffled by a long wet summer,
An unexpected break, another chance.

Across the Street

Across the street, their curtains are closed tight,
All day, all night, though people come and go:
A stubbly man who casts a cautious glance
Each way along the pavement; his plump wife
With boy or younger girl or blotchy dog –
Sometimes two of these, never all three.
Their door's always unlocked: they don't use keys.
And yet their house seems uninhabited:
Even that Friday night it gave a party,
All for itself, dancing to the foundations,
Or when slight shadows skim its glazed front door.

Across the street, they say: *Across the street,*
There's a man who keeps odd hours, who sits at home,
Hunched over a desk, or waves his arms about.
Odd parcels come by post; we've seen him too
Dashing to catch the five o'clock collection,
As if his so-called 'life' depended on it.
We think he drinks. His friends seem strange and few.

Across the street, I wonder if that's true.

Two Adolescents

They remind me, with their sloping shrugging gait,
Slack confidential chat, taking the dog
For its evening walk, these two, they remind me

Of warm September nights when we talked and talked
Until dawn brought us sleep. They remind me
Of the times I used to tell you everything.

At the End of the Line

with thanks to Olly

At the end of the line, there are ships nudging the quay.
There is water bluer than you might have imagined.

Commercial Road's terraces should gleam with colours
Borrowed from harbour lights: it could be Copenhagen.

Except, at the end of the line, the station windows are boarded.
The last train has gone. There are people shuffling in gutters.

Brave nautical statues shade their eyes against wasteland:
Tarnished Carr of the Ocean looks baffled by 'Cash 4 U',

And the smell of a fried past wafts over the swing bridge
With its unblinking message: *When red man shows wait HERE.*

And yes, at the end of the line, I am always waiting.
I am always waiting for you at the end of the line.

3

The Nature of Things

for Rod Shand

Polonius: What do you read, my lord?
Hamlet: Words, words, words.
                              Hamlet, II.2.191–2

Apple

An apple on a leafless branch in autumn holds the winter back;
As here, an Apple on the desk, my fruitful glowing Mac.

Books

Books are good to have around:
They decorate an empty space,
Lend graceless rooms a borrowed grace;
In noisy homes they deaden sound.

With what absurd self-consciousness
We handle them: the more we know,
The less we sense the way to show
Intuitive receptiveness.

The bibliophile's or scholar's need
To index, date, or cross-refer
Is always there to interfere
With what we once had: a good read.

Carcanet

*Car*canet? Car*can*et? Who could know
What it meant, how to pronounce the thing?
And who'd have guessed, those thirty years ago,
How many pearls would gather on its string?

Doves

Two collared doves feeding, their clockwork nods
    Discreetly out of synch:
One pecks demurely at a crust of bread,
    The other stops to drink,
As peaceable as legend decrees,
    Or so I choose to think.

Epigrams

Of epigrams (and epigraphs) beware:
They smile most charmingly before they snare.
Regard them as a double-sided cloak:
The sweetest grin conceals the sourest joke.

Of epigrams (not epigraphs) take heed:
Be sure that what you see is what you read;
For what you see may dance before your eyes,
But what you read will leave you old and wise.

Fog

Auden thanked you: now the thanks decay.
Gershwin too; though Billie Holiday
Transformed her foggy day in London town:
The sun (she sang) was shining upside-down.

Garden

My garden is bounded by an ancient wall,
Watched over by two towers, round Trinity
And square St Mary's, whose proximity
Informs its habits: knotty shrubs grow tall
And climbers grasp towards the crowded sky.

Hands

Scabbed and scratched by cooking, gardening,
And middle age's dim incompetence,
You have claimed unlooked-for independence.
You have become recalcitrant. You drop things.

And yet, hands, your skills are undiminished
Where most they matter. You manage a signature,
Most days, and can tackle an easy sonata.
You tie impenetrable knots. You are good in bed.

Ice

O for a muse of fire, or even ice,
Which would (as Robert Frost observed) suffice.

Jazz

Not blue. Deep green of Bechet's sad soprano;
Rich terracotta red of Satchmo's horn;
Steely violet glow of Parker's alto;
Ochres and sepias of Duke Ellington …

An old unfathomable love: now that's blue.

Key

That key you gave me years ago
Slept in a drawer, cocooned with dust;
Its blunted teeth were stained with rust.
Its function I no longer know.

Yet, far away, a slow clock ticks
And patient time comes circling back.
The sun turns through its zodiac.
The minutes pass. The lock unsticks.

Light

Light falls in its haphazard way,
Illuminates the here and there,
Enhances space, transfigures air.
It blunders in where shadows play.

The stunts it pulls as clouds roll by
Must always take us by surprise,
As scenes catch light before our eyes:
A Constable sea; a Turner sky.

Music

No, Pater, no:
All art does not aspire to its condition.
Haydn, Mozart, Schubert, Mahler, Britten
Speak what we cannot speak, beyond the sayable,
Translate the universe into the playable.
Our lesser arts must learn how to be humble.
And words? Just listen to them stumble.

Name

My name and I are not on speaking terms.
It owns an overdraft, a little fame,
A modest house, a car; yet all confirms
One sombre fact: I do not love my name.

And yet, why should I? That's for others, surely:
No earthly point becoming covetous
About a thing so near, so arbitrary!
Just watch yourself, as Zeus said to Narcissus.

Oaks

Bronze oaks stretch out against November sky.
They have sculpted their own trunks. They rule the fields:
They make the gangling pylons insecure.

I'd leave my bike near here and catch a lift
To school. Returning in the afternoon,
I'd often find the saddle acorn-strewn.

Those acorns, some of them, must be fine trees
By now, though merely twigs compared with these.

Irons Bottom

Prayer

Prayer came to me one autumn night
    In frosty Warwickshire:
I sought for words against the dark,
    Though whether God would hear

I hardly cared or guessed. That was
    Some half a life ago:
The habit formed, it captured me
    In its warm mist, and so

When I repeat the form of words,
    I God or self deceive,
For I have never ceased to pray
    Nor started to believe.

Quires

And yet, what is belief? I think of Sundays
When, long ago, we'd make the chancel ring
With our transfigured voices, and shall always
Be drawn to 'Quires and Places where they sing'.

Roads

Roads are linear, and so
You might expect them to be straight;
But roads both twist and deviate –
The back and forth, the high and low –

And seem perversely to avoid
The places signposts advertise,
Beguilingly, on either side.
Those villages that roads despise

Remain unvisited, unknown,
Unspoilt perhaps; for who can tell
Who travels, sadly and alone,
The tarmac lines from hell to hell?

Squib

A squib, you see, is what this is:
Too damp to spark, or even fizz.

Tracks

Tracks seen from the window of a moving train
Run with us brightly in parallel, then gradually
Fade, like old friends, from view. We glimpse them again,
Among nettles and willow-herb, neglected now and rusty,
Breaking under the strain of keeping up with us,
Until they reach their broken buffers, we our terminus.

Umbrage

I'd like to think that Umbrage
Is a posher sort of Uxbridge:
A spa wrapped in the Sussex Downs,
One letter south from other towns
Like Tunbridge Wells or Tonbridge,

Which ladies from Jane Austen
Could decorously get lost in.
To sip at its medicinal spring
Would prove the cure for anything:
They'd call it 'Taking Umbrage'.

Vanity

Ah, vanity: I remember
Posting off my masterpiece,
As an ambitious teenager,
To a firm in Southend on Sea
Which advertised in *Private Eye*.

I was the great discovery
Whom they'd be proud to publish,
If I'd just send them fifty quid.
I thought it better spent on drink.
A lesson learnt. I think.

Wheels are circular, and so
You might expect them to repeat
Some self-perpetuating feat;
But wheels engage with what's below.

Thus, unless a rocking pram
Should choreograph their static dance,
Wheels meet at each circumference
Newly charted tarmacadam.

The fascination of what's found
Meshes with known patterns turning,
Held at the hub, forever singing
The same song over different ground.

X

Skiving off rugby
One bleak afternoon,
I sneaked to the matinée
X at the Odeon.

In the side corridor,
I switched my school tie
Before reaching the foyer.
They took my money.

Just as it should be.

Youth

'And in my youth ...' 'Which youth was that?' you'll say,
'The one I saw you with the other day?'

Zero

What a bunch of no-hopers these tail-enders are
For anyone seeking an icon or hero:
There's whimsical Zeus, but elsewhere the score
Is sadly, emphatically, zilch, even zero.

4

Was and Is

I was the child who scarred his forehead
Riding his tricycle past an open window;
Who lied to doctors, dentists and opticians;
Whose feet defeated even Daniel Neal.

I was the child who fainted in assembly;
Who ran cross-country to be on my own;
Whose mind slid past classroom windows
To alight on tombstones, junkshops, sky.

I was the child who made a world in a shed;
Who talked to animals, birds and sunsets;
Who built an igloo from the first snowfall.
I am the man who is almost none the wiser.

The Picture of the Mind

for Peter Scupham

He meant of course 'the picture in the mind' –
Those images of origins and ends
That danced into a world he'd left behind –
But what's a preposition between friends?

'I cannot paint,' he said, 'what then I was';
And then he painted it. A nice conceit?
Or did the words seem vulnerable because
Such part-disclosure must be indiscreet?

If so, his indiscretions served him well:
For half-disclosing is what poems do,
In hints and emblems seeming to reveal
The picture of the mind – iambic, true.

Finzi's Orchard

There is special power in an adoptive landscape,
Unsmudged by ties of birth or ancestry,
Unburnished by false childhood memory.

Hampshire downland: Church Farm, Ashmansworth.
'This,' he said, 'is what I have always longed for.'
Not meaning, I think, anything as easy

As an edenic ideal, but rather the place
To do what he did best: to cultivate
Rare apple trees, collect rare poets, write

An English music – more than English because
His outsider's eye and ear have given it
Such frail disenchantment, such haunted repose.

Shakespeare, Milton, Traherne, Wordsworth, Hardy:
Their words are kerned, finding new edges,
New spaces between them, and new purity

Of diction. There is fresh wind in the trees;
A russet windfall nestles in the grass;
The russet clarinet rests on its bed of strings.

Three Sightings of W.G. Sebald

1

In the Jolly Sailor, you prod at skate and chips,
Having just been ferried back from 'the island' –
Now visitable though not demystified.
There's strange abandonedness at Shingle Street,
But nowhere hugs its secrecy like this.
You look weary. Skate's a difficult fish.

2

In the Jubilee Hall, you read from *The Rings of Saturn*
As if you'd written it in English; are coy
About translators. The first questioner wants to know
Why the pages of his copy have come loose.
Tonight, a Brendel concert at the Maltings:
These twinkling Germanic melancholics!

3

In the darkest corner of a Bungay junkshop,
You carefully leaf through the sepia postcards
As if they tell your story: which they do.
These images meld into narrative;
The narrative enacts your images.
Mind-traveller, time-traveller, you are the alchemist.

Adam

Be with me, quiet ghost, as the short days lengthen,
As blackthorn winter staggers into spring:
Where my resolves are weakest, you will strengthen.

Be with me, quiet ghost, as the long days shorten,
And light begins its slow unravelling:
Where my resolves are slackest, you will tauten.

My friend, my reader, you are still nearby,
Your wry wise presence undiminishing:
Be with me, quiet ghost, as the seasons die.

Thanks

I.O.J.P. 1911–1994

And you thought I'd forgotten. Hardly. It's just
that the book's last poem had to be for you,
made of these stammering, rueful syllabics,
the closest thing that poets have to silence.
Though in truth I shan't forget our silences:
yours, as I thought, fraught with disdain and distance,
mine full of priggish intellectual anger –
a line of communication, after all,
since in the end we knew each other too well
to need to speak.
           Outside, slow November dusk:
this is the moment we depressives like best,
when jabbering daylight no longer nags at us
and melancholia makes us feel at home;
time to close curtains, get the tea, look forward
to sherry, supper and a long safe evening;
then crossword, concert on the Third, a nightcap,
and who's to worry if we should fall asleep?
Knowing this, one might be inclined to wonder
how you put up with the years in the City,
the office, the trains, the European trips
to glass factories where they never rumbled
your consummate disguise. But I did. Even
on holiday, you'd do your best, as homesick
as Mr Woodhouse.
           Like me, you loathed summer:
ill at ease on beaches, though fond of cricket.
Saturday mornings, whatever the season,
you came into your own – the sort of father
every boy wants, and somehow all the better
for being that special weekend creation:
we were let loose, while mother shopped in Reigate,
on our equal, comradely exploration –
Finch's cycle shop; or, up a steep alley,
beyond the Town Hall, La Trobe's model railways;
Forte's ice-cream at Mrs Lee's in Bell Street;

and doughnuts to take home for elevenses.
Yes, you indulged me, by indulging yourself:
were seldom, I now think, happier.
                                    Of course,
it couldn't last: that's childhood for you. Going
away to school, I lost you: it had to be,
for the son whom you wanted to have everything
you'd lacked in your education couldn't be
the son who'd follow you into the business,
who was also the son you wanted; besides,
that barely imagined public school turned out
to be one where masters read the *Guardian*
and talked about Sartre. Soon I'd be writing home
to declare myself an 'interlectual':
you simply corrected the spelling, as when
'This is a wasted stamp, this a waisted stamp',
followed by one stuck uselessly on the page
and another with neat cuts to its middle,
put me right on that score.
                                    I kept on learning
from you longer than you guessed: as a student
in the silly, permissive nineteen-sixties –
literary, leftish, decidedly queer –
I'd still wear jacket and tie to seminars,
in tepid debates invoke Uncle Enoch,
kinship his Brummie vowels made unlikely,
though sure to fire the rebels of '68!
(What's worse, or better, I surmised even then
that one reason they couldn't stomach Powell
was his wry assumption that they'd read Virgil.)
You admired his intransigent honesty –
and yes, so did I, shameless contrarian,
my father's son.
                                    Contrarians don't get on,
unless they negotiate a steady truce,
which we didn't. Should we have done? I doubt it.
Awkwardly different yet exactly alike
was how we were planned to be, if there's a plan,
yet there were times when each might have intervened:
I should have urged you to take more exercise,
and you should have talked me out of starting that

ridiculous bookshop. There'd have been no point:
when either of us knew we were being daft,
we'd only grow more obstinate.

                            Still, I don't know
whether you ever reached where you were going;
whether at last in Orford you were happy;
whether you were proud – or not ashamed – of me.
'You can't do better than your best' you'd tell me,
but so often I've not done that. It's dark now,
freezing hard outside, another winter's night,
as I write these lines: they're not the half of it.
If reading is what completes a poem, then
of course this poem can never be complete:
all it can edge or stumble towards is what,
holding your hand for the first time since childhood,
at that June lunchtime in a hospital room,
I tried to whisper but you quite understood.
Thanks. And that indeed is what I meant to say.